THE GREENBRIER GHOST

A GHOST CONVICTS HER KILLER

BY MEGAN ATWOOD

CAPSTONE PRESS
a capstone imprint

Snap Books is published by Capstone Press, an imprint of Capstone.
1710 Roe Crest Drive
North Mankato, Minnesota 56003
www.capstonepub.com

Library of Congress Cataloging-in-Publication Data is available on the Library of Congress website.

ISBN: 978-1-5435-7339-8 (hardcover)
ISBN: 978-1-4966-6612-3 (paperback)
ISBN: 978-1-5435-7348-0 (eBook PDF)

Summary: Elva Zona Heaster died in Greenbrier County, West Virginia, in January 1897. Her death was originally thought to be from natural causes. But when Zona's ghost began visiting her mother, the death began to look a lot more suspicious. This terrifying true story details the trial of Zona's murderer and the evidence presented against him from Zona herself, beyond the grave.

Image Credits
Associated Press: Jon C. Hancock, 27; Brittany Wykle: 29; iStockphoto: atosan, 20; Library of Congress: Carol M. Highsmith Archive, 10; Shutterstock: Anthony Ricci, 14-15, avtk, Design Element, Chantal de Bruijne, Design Element, Constantine Pankin, 23, Drpixel, 7, Evgeniia Litovchenko, Cover, Giraphics, Design Element, GoMixer, Design Element, Igor Normann, 9, Lario Tus, 5, 25, MagicDogWorkshop, Design Element, NikhomTreeVector, Design Element, Paul McKinnon, 13, pterwort, 8, Tom Tom, 18, VitalyRomanovich, 16

Editorial Credits
Editor: Eliza Leahy; Designers: Lori Bye and Brann Garvey;
Media Researcher: Tracy Cummins; Production Specialist: Kathy McColley

Direct Quotations
Page 10: https://www.americanhauntingsink.com/greenbrier?rq=shue
Pages 22, 26: https://wvpentours.com/about/history/articles/the-greenbrier-ghost/
Page 24: http://www.wvculture.org/history/crime/shuearticles.html

All internet sites appearing in front and back matter were available and accurate when this book was sent to press.

Printed and bound in the USA. PA99

TABLE OF CONTENTS

A VISIT FROM BEYOND

Mary Jane Heaster knew her daughter's death on January 23, 1897, was no accident. She had proof. She just needed to convince the **prosecutor**, John Alfred Preston, to reopen the case.

Mary Jane visited John's office to speak with him. She was armed with the perfect reason the case should be reopened.

The conversation lasted for hours. But finally, the prosecutor agreed to investigate more. Mary Jane left the office and waited for the investigation to start.

How did she know for sure the death was suspicious? Her dead daughter, Elva Zona Heaster Shue, had told her. Zona's ghost had visited Mary Jane four nights in a row to tell her how she died. And just as Mary Jane had suspected, Zona's death was no accident.

It was murder.

SKEPTIC'S NOTE

Skeptics might believe that Mary Jane Heaster had been having **hallucinations**. There is no proof that Zona appeared in ghost form other than her mother's account.

CHAPTER ONE

SWEPT OFF HER FEET

Elva Zona Heaster had lived in rural West Virginia from birth. Born around 1873 in Greenbrier County, Zona led a pretty ordinary life. That is, until she met Erasmus Stribbling Trout Shue.

In October 1896, Trout had been moving from town to town, looking for a new life and work. He had just landed in Greenbrier County, where he found work as a **blacksmith**. There, he met young Zona. She fell madly in love with him.

FACT

Birth certificates weren't used as a standard practice in the United States until after 1945! Many people didn't know the date of their actual birth.

But Zona's mother disapproved. Mary Jane Heaster had a feeling Trout Shue was bad news.

That didn't stop Zona. She and Trout had a **whirlwind** romance. Only two weeks after they'd met, on October 20, 1896, Zona and Trout got married. Zona thought she'd found the perfect person for her.

She didn't know that their romance would come to an abrupt end only three months later.

A TERRIBLE END

On January 23, 1897, Trout Shue was working at the blacksmith shop. He **allegedly** sent a neighbor boy, Andy Jones, to his and Zona's house to run an errand. When Andy arrived, he found Zona's body. She lay at the bottom of the stairs inside her house. The boy ran to tell his mother and then Trout what he'd seen. The local doctor, Dr. George W. Knapp, was summoned.

When Dr. Knapp arrived at the house, Zona's body wasn't at the bottom of the stairs. Trout had come home and moved her body up to the second-floor bedroom. He had dressed Zona in a high-necked dress, which he said was for burial.

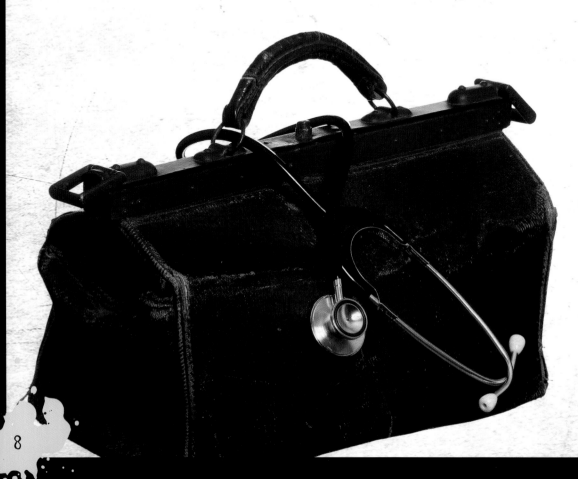

Zona was wearing a high-necked dress for burial. Some people thought Trout did this to mask the bruising on her neck.

Dr. Knapp saw that Zona was dead. But when he tried to examine Zona, Trout cradled her head and sobbed. Dr. Knapp noticed some bruising on Zona's neck. When he tried to get a closer look, Trout lashed out at him. The doctor ended the examination early because of Trout's grief. He later wrote that the cause of Zona's death was an "everlasting faint."

SKEPTIC'S NOTE

Dr. Knapp couldn't seem to decide on a cause of death. At first he ruled Zona's death an "everlasting faint"—what we would call a heart attack today. Dr. Knapp later said Zona's death was due to childbirth. There were no reports that Zona had been pregnant, though. Because of this, all his judgments about Zona's death seem uncertain.

CHAPTER TWO

A BAD GUY

When Mary Jane found out about her daughter's death, her first words were, "The devil has killed her!" She had no doubt that Trout had been the cause of Zona's death. She knew he wasn't who he pretended to be.

The West Virginia State Penitentiary, where Trout served time, operated from 1876–1995.

A TROUBLED PAST

Mary Jane had been right. Trout was born in Augusta County, Virginia, around 1861. He had been in and out of trouble his whole life. He'd been in jail for several different crimes, ranging from theft to **assault**.

Trout had also been married twice before. Both marriages had ended badly. The first marriage to Allie Estelline Cutlip ended in divorce. The reason? Cruelty. Trout's cruelty to his first wife had been recorded as the reason for the end of the marriage.

In fact, in one story, Trout had been so cruel to Allie that neighbors went to Trout's house and threw him into the river in the dead of winter. Clearly, people found Trout's treatment of his wife disturbing. When Trout was convicted for stealing horses, Allie took the opportunity to file for divorce.

FACT

Prison systems in the 1800s were often harsh. Prisoners had to work long, hard days—sometimes fifteen hours a day!

Even more disturbing was Trout's second marriage. Trout's second wife, Lucy Ann Tritt, died mysteriously. Only eight months into their marriage, Lucy was found dead. The cause of death was unclear.

Accounts of her "accidental" death ranged from her slipping on ice, to being hit on the head, to dying by poison. No one knew exactly how she died. But many people suspected Trout had had something to do with it.

Mary Jane Heaster's hunch about Trout seemed to be true.

SUSPICIOUS BEHAVIOR

Other people found Trout's behavior after Zona's death suspicious as well. Trout refused to leave her side, even when the **undertakers** came to move her. Trout seemed to be really worried about her head and neck. He shielded them from view of others.

Mary Jane Heaster thought Trout's actions were those of a guilty man. She wanted another investigation. But she had no real reason to ask for one except for her feelings. She needed something more.

SKEPTIC'S NOTE

Can you tell if someone is guilty of murder by their behavior? Not really. People **grieve** in many different ways and sometimes have strange reactions to **trauma** or loss.

FUNERALS IN THE 1800S

In the Victorian era, mourning for a loved one was something people did in public. **Visitations** lasted for three or four days. In Appalachia, often when a person died a local church bell would toll. Then the family would "lay the body out" to get it ready for the wake and burial. Family and friends would wash the body. They dressed the person in their best clothes. Sometimes a burial bedsheet, known as a shroud, would be used to cover the body. Then there would be a "sitting up." During this time, people would visit the family and the body. Visitors would sing songs. They would bring food. And they would speak about their faith. This helped families to grieve for their loved ones.

A SIGN

After Zona was buried, Mary Jane tried to return the burial bedsheet to Trout. He refused to take it. Mary Jane took it home with her and tried to wash it. The minute the sheet hit the water, the water turned red. Then the bedsheet turned pink. The red color in the water disappeared, but the stain on the bedsheet would not go away.

Mary Jane took this as a sign that Zona's death was truly not an accident. She prayed with all her might that Zona would somehow let her know what had really happened.

Some people say the statue of Benjamin Franklin at the front of the American Philosophical Society Library comes to life and dances on the city streets.

FAMOUS GHOSTS

In the United States, some famous ghosts have haunted people for years. In Philadelphia, the ghost of Benjamin Franklin, inventor and Founding Father, is said to haunt the American Philosophical Society Library. People believe he roams the city at night. Abraham Lincoln's ghost has been spotted both in the White House and outside the Springfield, Illinois, state capitol. And Mark Twain, an author, has been seen outside his former apartment building in New York City.

CHAPTER THREE

GHOSTS DON'T LIE

Mary Jane didn't have to wait long for her prayers to be answered. Several weeks after her daughter's funeral, a mysterious bright light shone near Mary Jane's bed while she slept. She awoke and sat up quickly, scared. The light dimmed. The temperature in the room dropped suddenly.

She saw it was the ghost of her daughter, Zona. Despite how scared she was, Mary Jane listened to what Zona had to say.

ARE GHOSTS REAL?

Ghosts are said to be spirits of humans (and sometimes animals) who are left behind after they die. But if you think you've seen a ghost, there might be some other explanation for it. Here are some examples:

• Have you ever felt like there was something in the room with you, even if you couldn't see it? This could be from an electromagnetic field nearby. Some scientists think that these fields interact with people's brains, causing them to see or feel things that aren't really there.

• A not-so-fun reason you might feel you've seen a ghost is from mold. Mold has been known to cause irrational fear, loss of memory, and balance problems.

• Another not-so-fun reason you might have seen a ghost? Carbon monoxide poisoning. This type of poisoning in the air can cause people to have hallucinations.

FACT

One of the first ghost stories ever recorded in the Western world came from Pliny the Younger, an ancient Roman author and statesman. He wrote about an old man draped in chains who terrorized residents in a rental house in Athens.

Zona had a lot to say. For four nights, Zona allegedly visited her mother and told her what had happened. She told Mary Jane about how cruel Trout had been during their short marriage. He had been mean and hurtful. He lashed out at Zona for no reason at all. Sometimes he would hurt her physically.

THE FATEFUL NIGHT

On the night of Zona's death, Trout had been in one of his moods. Zona's ghost told her mother that she had cooked Trout dinner like usual that night. But Trout grew angry when he thought Zona hadn't cooked any meat for dinner. He flew into a rage and choked her to death.

Zona's ghost could even prove that her neck had been broken. As a frightened Mary Jane watched, Zona turned her head all the way around. Mary Jane knew she had been right. Her daughter's death had not been an accident—it was murder. And Trout had been the one to murder her. Now Mary Jane just had to convince everyone else.

FACT

According to a 2017 survey, around 45 percent of people in the United States believe ghosts are real!

A MOTHER'S MISSION

Mary Jane marched to the prosecutor, John Alfred Preston. She told him all about Zona's visits. After many hours, Mary Jane finally convinced Preston to reopen the case. As part of his investigation, Preston talked to Dr. Knapp about the medical examination. The doctor admitted it hadn't been as thorough as he wanted. The case was reopened. Zona's body was **exhumed** for an **autopsy**.

Sure enough, the autopsy showed that Zona's story seemed to be true. Her neck had been broken. She had bruises in the shapes of fingers wrapped around it. It became clear that someone was responsible for Zona's death. And that someone seemed more and more likely to be Trout.

People who had gone to Zona's visitation talked about Trout's strange behavior. One moment he would sob noisily. To some, this seemed over the top—like he was pretending. In the next moment, he would shoo people away from Zona wildly. Some people wondered if he didn't want people to see her neck and the bruises on it. When they looked into Zona's coffin, investigators found that Trout had wedged her head between a pillow and the side of the coffin so that her neck would look straight.

With this new information, the prosecutor had enough to charge Trout with Zona's murder.

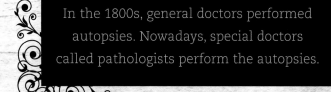

FACT

In the 1800s, general doctors performed autopsies. Nowadays, special doctors called pathologists perform the autopsies.

CHAPTER FOUR

THE TRIAL

Trout was charged with Zona's murder, and law enforcement arrested him. Trout simply didn't believe he could be convicted. He allegedly said to others both in and out of jail, "They will not be able to prove I did it."

However, Preston set out to do just that. But there was a problem. He didn't have any direct **evidence** that Trout had killed Zona. What he did have was some observations and the word of a ghost. Still, he knew that Mary Jane would make a great witness. So he put her on the stand.

FACT

"Direct evidence" means something that links a person to a crime. If someone saw a person commit a crime, their **testimony** would be direct evidence.

GHOSTLY TESTIMONY

In June 1897, Mary Jane took an **oath** to tell the truth. The prosecutor decided not to question her about Zona's ghostly visits. He worried that the judge and jury would think she was foolish.

But for this same reason, the defense attorney decided to question her about the ghost. He hoped her stories about Zona's ghost would convince the jury that she was insane.

Mary Jane stood before the court and described Zona's visits in detail. She told the jury what her daughter had said. Mary Jane recounted how Trout was angry about the dinner Zona had cooked him. He was so angry he got violent.

Nearing the end of her story, Mary Jane said of Zona's ghost: "She cames [sic] four times, and four nights; but the second night she told me that her neck was squeezed off at the first joint and it was just as she told me."

After Mary Jane had told the jury all about Zona's visits, the defense attorney tried to make her sound even more foolish. He asked, "Mrs. Heaster, are you positively sure that these are not four dreams?"

Mary Jane answered, "Yes, sir. It was not a dream. I don't dream when I am wide awake, to be sure; and I know I saw her right there with me."

SKEPTIC'S NOTE

Even before the marriage, Mary Jane admitted that she didn't like Trout. After Zona died, Mary Jane might have assumed Trout had murdered her. This would confirm what she already believed—that he was no good. This is called "confirmation bias." Confirmation bias is when a person embraces information that confirms what they already believe and rejects anything that doesn't support what they believe (or want to believe).

CHAPTER FIVE

CONVICTION

When Mary Jane was done, it was Trout's turn to tell his tale. He rambled aimlessly and talked for an entire afternoon.

The newspaper *Greenbrier Independent* stated that he made an "unfavorable impression" on the spectators. They reported that he described unimportant things. He denied everything the witnesses said. When he was done, he challenged the jury to "Look into my face and say I am guilty." The jury was unmoved. Much like his actions at the visitation, he just didn't seem like he was telling the truth.

His words from prison also came back to haunt him. He'd told a fellow prisoner that he had a lifelong goal of having seven wives. The information about Trout's first two wives also came out. Finally, what he had told a fellow inmate made him sound even guiltier to the jury: "They will not be able to prove I did it."

Compared to Mary Jane Heaster, Trout Shue didn't sound trustworthy at all.

SKEPTIC'S NOTE

If someone isn't good at speaking in court, it doesn't mean they're guilty. Trout could have just been bad at testifying.

The Greenbrier County courthouse, where Trout was tried, is located in Lewisburg, West Virginia.

Trout's defense lawyers tried to paint Mary Jane Heaster as crazy. After all, who would admit to seeing a ghost, let alone getting the real story from one? But her steadfast answers and unwavering belief seemed to be enough for the jury.

After only 70 minutes of deliberation, the jury came back with the **verdict**. Trout Shue was found guilty. He was convicted of murdering his wife, Elva Zona Heaster Shue.

The judge sentenced him to life in prison. But in March 1900, less than three years after his conviction, Trout Shue died.

Although Mary Jane had been frightened by her daughter's ghostly visits, she found a way to make sure Zona's voice was heard—even if it was from beyond the grave.

FACT

This is the only time in United States history that testimony from a ghost was admitted to court as evidence.

Zona's grave can still be found in the graveyard of Soule Methodist Church.

IN MEMORY OF
ZONA HEASTER
SHUE
"GREENBRIER GHOST"
1876 — 1897

GLOSSARY

allegedly (ah-LEHJ-ehd-lee)—according to some people, but not a fact

assault (uh-SAWLT)—to attack someone physically

autopsy (AWE-tahp-see)—an examination of a body after death

blacksmith (BLAK-smihth)—a person who makes and repairs things in iron

evidence (EH-vih-dehns)—facts and/or information that is true

exhume (ek-ZOOM)—to unbury a body

grieve (GREEV)—to feel intense sorrow

hallucination (huh-LOO-sih-nay-shun)—a vision of something that isn't really there

oath (OHTH)—a formal promise or declaration

prosecutor (PRAH-seh-kyoo-ter)—an attorney who tries to convict a defendant of a crime

skeptic (SKEP-tihk)—someone who doubts or questions beliefs

testimony (TEST-ih-moh-nee)—statements made under oath during a trial or legal proceeding

trauma (TRAH-mah)—a physical injury or an intensely distressing experience

undertaker (UHN-dur-tay-kur)—a person whose job is to prepare dead bodies for burial and to arrange funerals

verdict (VUR-dikt)—a decision or judgment made by a jury

visitation (viz-ih-TAY-shun)—a time when friends and family come to view a person who has died and to gain comfort from one another

whirlwind (WURL-wind)—happening very quickly

READ MORE

Chandler, Matt. *Famous Ghost Stories of North America*. North Mankato, MN: Capstone Press, 2019.

Giannini, Alex. *Frightening Farmhouses*. New York: Bearport Publishing Company, Inc., 2019.

Kovacs, Vic. *Haunted Towns and Villages*. New York: Crabtree Publishing Company, 2018.

INTERNET SITES

Ghost-Hunting Gadgets

https://www.npr.org/2011/10/31/141868232/paranormal-technology-gadgets-for-ghost-tracking

More About the Greenbrier Ghost

https://www.youtube.com/watch?v=uDpBKDK56EI

Things You Didn't Know About Ghosts

https://www.cbc.ca/kidscbc2/the-feed/monsters-101-all-about-ghosts

INDEX